Nazim Hikmet

RUBAIYAT

Translated by Randy Blasing and Mutlu Konuk

Copper Beech Press

The publication of this book was made possible by a grant from the National Endowment for the Arts, a Federal agency, in Washington, D.C.

Cover: 13th-Century Stone Relief, Seljuk Museum, Konya, Turkey.

Copyright© 1985 by Randy Blasing and Mutlu Konuk
All rights reserved.
For information, address the publisher:
> Copper Beech Press
> P.O.Box 2578
> Providence, Rhode Island 02906

Library of Congress Cataloging in Publication Data
Nâzim Hikmet, 1902-1963.
  Rubáiyát.

  Translation of Rubailer.
  I. Blasing, Randy. II. Blasing, Mutlu Konuk,
1944-   . III. Title.
PS248.H45R813   1985   894'.3513   85-15151
ISBN 0-914278-48-7 (pbk. : alk. paper)

Third Printing
Printed in the United States of America

Acknowledgments

Grateful acknowledgment is made to the editors of the magazines in which the contents of this book originally appeared, often in slightly different form:

The American Poetry Review: "First Series (5, 13)"
The Antioch Review: "Third Series"
Ararat: "Fourth Series"
The Literary Review: "Second Series"
Translation: "First Series (1-4, 6-12)"

Contents

First Series	11
Second Series	27
Third Series	35
Fourth Series	41
Afterword	49

First Series

1

The world you saw was real, Rumi, not an Apparition, etc.
It is endless and uncreated, its Painter is not the First Cause, etc.
And the greatest of the rubáiyát your burning flesh left us
is not the one that goes, "All Forms are shadows," etc. . . .

2

My soul neither was before she was, nor attains to a mystery that isn't she:
my soul is an image of her, she the image of the outside world reflected in me.
And the image farthest from and closest to its original
is my love's beauty illuminating me. . .

3

My love's image in the mirror had its say:
"She is not—I am," it said to me one day.
I struck, the mirror shattered, the image disappeared
but, thank goodness, my love stayed. . .

4

I painted you on canvas only once,
but I picture you a thousand times a day.
Amazingly, your image there will last:
the canvas has a longer life than I. . .

5

I can't kiss and make love with your image,
but there in my city you're flesh and blood,
and your red mouth, the honey I'm denied, your big eyes, really are,
and your surrender like rebel waters, your whiteness I can't even touch. . .

6

She kissed me: "These lips are real like the universe," she said.
"This fragrance isn't your invention, it's the spring in my hair," she said.
"Watch them in the sky or in my eyes:
the blind may not see them, but the stars are there," she said. . .

7

This garden, this moist earth, this jasmine scent, this moonlit night
will sparkle still when I've passed from the light,
because it was before I came, and afterwards wasn't part of me—
a mere copy of this original appeared in me. . .

8

One day Mother Nature will say, "Quitting time—
    no more laughter or tears, my child. . ."
And endless once again it will begin:
    life that does not see, speak, or think. . .

9

Separation draws closer each day:
good-bye, my beautiful world,
and hello,
        u n i v e r s e . . .

10

Full honeycomb—
I mean, your eyes full of sun. . .
Your eyes, my love, will be dust tomorrow,
the honey will fill other combs. . .

11

They're neither light
                nor clay,
my love, her cat, and the bead on his collar:
it's all in the kneading, the dough is the same...

12

Cabbage, car, plague germ, star:
we're all kith and kin.
Not, my sun-eyed love, *"Cogito ergo sum"*
but, in our distinguished family, we can think because we are. . .

13

Just a difference of degree between us—
that's how it is, my canary:
you with wings, an unthinking bird,
and me with hands, a thinking man. . .

Second Series

1

"Fill your cup with wine before your cup fills with dust," said Khayyám.
A man with a bony nose and no shoes stared at him in his rose garden:
"In a world with more blessings than stars," he said, "I'm starving,
I don't have enough money to buy bread, let alone wine..."

2

To think with sweet sorrow on death and life's brevity,
to drink wine in a tulip garden by moonlight...
Our whole life, we never felt this sweet sorrow
in the cellar of a coal-black house, at city's end...

3

Life is passing—seize time's bounty before you sleep the unwaking sleep:
fill the crystal goblet with ruby wine—young man, it's dawn, awake...
In his bare, ice-cold room the young man awoke:
it was the shrieking factory whistle, and it didn't forgive being late...

4

I don't miss days gone by
    —except one summer night—
and even the last blue sparkle of my eyes
    will flash you news of days to come. . .

5

I, one man,
the Turkish poet Nazim Hikmet, me—
faith from head to toe,
from head to toe struggle and hope—that's me. . .

6

I, the announcer, speak,
my voice grave and naked like a seed:
I'm setting the time of my heart,
at the tone it will be dawn...

Third Series

1

Either people love you
or they're your enemy.
Either you're forgotten as if you didn't exist,
or you're not out of mind for a moment...

2

Clear as glass, an unspoiled winter day—
to bite into the firm white flesh of a healthy apple!
My love, it's like the joy of breathing
in a snowy pine forest, this loving you. . .

3

Who knows, we might not have loved each other so
if we couldn't watch each other from afar.
Who knows, if fate hadn't separated us
we might never have been so close. . .

4

Night pales, day breaks.
Like water settling, everything grows clear, transparent.
My love, it's as if we suddenly came face to face:
all I see is light, light. . .

Fourth Series

1

To conquer lies in the heart, in books, and in the street,
in mothers' lullabies, in the announcer's news;
to know—it's a great happiness, my love—
to know what's past and what's to come...

2

Our arms are branches heavy with fruit:
the enemy shakes and shakes us,
and the better to harvest our fruit
they don't chain our feet, they fetter our minds. . .

3

As long as you love
and love as much as you can,
as long as you give your all to your love
and give as much as you can, you are young. . .

4

I think of Yahya Kemal, the Ottomans' poet laureate:
I see him in a store window, looking fat and pained.
And for some reason I suddenly think
of lame Byron dying in the Greek mountains. . .

5

I am a patient gardener,
you are my rose that blooms every seven years.
I don't lose heart because you are so rare—
I think that may be why you are so dear. . .

6

In this business you must be hard and a little proud:
not cruelty, grief, or sorrow
but death alone
               must see you surrender. . .

7

I don't mean to boast but
I've shot through ten years of bondage like a bullet.
And aside from the ache in my liver
my heart is still the same heart, my head still the same head...

Afterword

Nazim Hikmet began writing his rubáiyát in December 1945, in the eighth year of a twenty-eight-year sentence as a political prisoner. In a letter to his wife, Pirayé, he outlines his plans: "I've begun a new book—'Rubáiyát for Pirayé.' It will have about forty quatrains. I'm going to try something that's never been done in Western or Eastern literature—that is, put dialectical materialism into the rubáiyát form. And I'll succeed. Because your love will enable me to do the exact opposite of what Rumi's love of God inspired him to do." By January 1946 he had projected four series of rubáiyát: the first would be primarily philosophical, the second social, the third explicitly lyric, and the fourth mainly satirical.

The technical issue of adapting a traditional form to new content preoccupied Hikmet from the start. In a letter to Pirayé's son, Memet Fuat, he suggests that the original form served as a model for him: "True poets, those who have mastered their art, never write without some kind of measure or rhyme—even though they may deny it themselves—because if they did, they would be writing prose. In writing quatrains, rhyme is important, because rubáiyát—even the most philosophical or lyrical of them—are a species of polemical, didactic weapons in poetry. They must be easily memorized; they must be economically phrased. The classical rhyme scheme [*aaba*] makes all this possible. But sometimes a modern use of rhyme may be substituted for the classical scheme." In his first few rubáiyát, he reports, he worked to retain the classical form and manner as sort of a tuning-up exercise; subsequently, he experimented with new forms in order to accommodate his new content.

In the opening quatrains of the first series, Hikmet challenges the Neo-Platonism of the Sufi mystic poet Rumi (1207-1273), who lived in Konya in Turkey and founded the order of whirling dervishes. The entire first series becomes a running materialist critique of idealism, including Descartes' version (I, 12). The second series plays variations on the rubáiyát of the twelfth-century Persian poet Omar Khayyám and criticizes his hedonism from a socially conscious point of view. By coming to terms with such illustrious poetic predecessors, Hikmet claims his place in the Middle Eastern tradition in order to legitimize his revision—increasingly drastic as the series proceed—of both the form and the religious, philosophical, and social thinking historically associated with rubáiyát.